The Rt Revd John Eastaugh, Bishop of Hereford 1974-1990.
Painted in oil on panel by Daphne Todd, R.P., N.E.A.C., 1988.
Commissioned by the diocese.

THE BISHOPS OF HEREFORD AND THEIR PALACE

R. W. D. Fenn & J. B. Sinclair

Published by the Friends of Hereford Cathedral

Hereford 1990

For The Right Reverend John Richard Gordon Eastaugh
Bishop of Hereford 1974-1990

ISBN 0 904642 08 9

Printed by Orphans Press Ltd., Leominster, Herefordshire. Tel. 2460.

PREFACE

Prebendary A. L. Moir published the second edition of his *The Bishop's Palace Hereford* in 1976. Since then, however, our knowledge of some periods of the palace's history has been increased by archaeology and historical research. When the late bishop of Hereford, the Rt. Revd. John Eastaugh, invited us to revise Prebendary Moir's work for a third edition it soon became apparent that the result was going to be so very different from its predecessor, which was none the less its inspiration, that it did not deserve to carry its name. So, whilst gratefully acknowledging our debt to Prebendary Moir's work, we offer *The Bishops of Hereford and their palace* as a new interpretation of the history of the most important domestic building in the city of Hereford.

'The palace ... does not make a show. Its façade consists of various parts, first one of brick, gabled and apparently Victorian, then a neo-Norman porch, probably of the Cottingham time, then five bays of two storied, sashed Georgian brick, and then a projecting recent wing.'[1] Consequently, on coming through the gatehouse into the palace yard the first reaction is of slight disappointment: one *expects* a bishop's palace to make a show. But instead of spectacle one is offered architectural charm; comeliness rather than pretension. The effect is the same from the garden or eastern side of the palace. Once again, set amongst its spacious lawns and handsome trees, the Wye flowing beyond, the palace does not make a show, but creates in its architectural diversity a pleasing aesthetic unity: 'Georgian centre, stone-faced with sash windows on one and two floors, and a later gabled bay on the right. On the left and round the corner to the south ... it is Victorian brick with gables.'[2]

This pleasing aesthetic unity, however, was not achieved by accident or coincidence, but by a long succession of episcopal tenants who, each in their own way, accommodated the house to their own needs. In this sense few left it as they found it and in chronicling its history one has to look at them and their part in shaping its history. For this reason we have adopted the title *The Bishops of Hereford and their palace,* for the building can not be considered apart from those who lived in it.

We gratefully acknowledge the assistance we have had from Miss Penelope Morgan, MA, FRHistS, FLA, Librarian of the Cathedral Library, Miss Meryl Jancy, MA, Cathedral Archivist, Mr C. P. Canton, the Bishoprics Secretary of the Church Commissioners, Mr M. A. Faraday, Mr Basil Butcher of Hereford, Miss Joan Bookham, Honorary Secretary of The Friends of Hereford Cathedral, and, of course, the Bishop of Hereford himself who proved to be not only most patient and hospitable during our investigations of his home, but also disconcertingly knowledgeable. Intended to commemorate his retirement, now, in gratitude to his kindness and in sorrow at his death before this small book was published, we dedicate it to his memory.

Kington, February, 1990

CONTENTS

ILLUSTRATIONS

The Palace from the courtyard, showing the Romanesque porch and the 18th Century frontage. The roof line is that of the medieval palace.

I. THE BEGINNINGS

The origins of Christianity in Herefordshire are Celtic. They are earlier than the Saxon settlement of the area and belong to the sixth century.[3] But by the early eighth century Hereford was established as the ecclesiastical centre of the Magonsaete, a people who were predominantly Welsh in blood and speech and who occupied what became known as Herefordshire and southern Shropshire. The rise of Penda saw their incorporation into Mercia and the bishopric of Hereford acquired an important role in border politics which endured well into the Middle Ages. This is evidenced by one of its earliest bishops bearing the name Walhstod, meaning an interpreter, a necessary skill in a border diocese where Welsh as well as English was a language of both people and their princes. Consequently, the bishop's palace at Hereford from its earliest days had an important secular role in the life of the Welsh border. Its character was probably more Celtic than Roman and its pattern of life monastic and austere and perhaps not dissimilar to that of the bishop of St Davids, whose monks we are told pulled the plough as oxen themselves and drank nothing stronger than water.

No trace of this original Anglo-Celtic bishop's palace nor of its pre-Norman successors has survived. But excavation and street patterns have revealed the rectilinear shape of the eighth or ninth century Saxon burgh of Hereford within which the site occupied by the present cathedral and palace suggests it is in an area assigned for their predecessors from the outset. Life in these early palaces was often precarious and their proximity to the castle a mixed blessing. Thus the Welsh *Chronicle of the Princes* records that 'Seven hundred and sixty was the year of Christ when an encounter took place between the Britons and the Saxons in the battle of Hereford.' The place-name Hereford, commemorating an army ford, a ford where a marching column could pass, in closed order,[4] implies a potential for conflict and troubled times. In 926 Athelstan, king of Wessex, summoned the leading Welsh princes to Hereford and imposed a tribute upon them of gold, silver, cattle, hunting dogs and hawks and fixed the Wye as the boundary between the two races. But it gave the region little stability and when another Athelstan became bishop in 1012 he defined and put on record his diocesan boundaries where they met those of Worcester and acquired an estate of five hides at Inkberrow in Worcestershire which he bought for ten pounds of gold and silver.[5] He rebuilt his ruinous cathedral and, no doubt, the condition of the palace was little better. But neither the rebuilding of the cathedral nor, if it was attempted, that of the palace was to endure, for on 24th October, 1055 Gruffydd ap Llywelyn, who had established himself as master of all Wales, in company with Aelfgar, the aggrieved earl of Mercia, marched upon Hereford, taking the castle and giving the city over to fire and plunder. Not even Athelstan's new cathedral was spared. It was stripped of its relics and vestments, though seven of its canons died in its defence and Gruffydd 'with vast spoil and booty, returned to his land happily victorious.'[6] It is more than unlikely that the palace survived this onslaught unscathed.

Bishop Athelstan died in the following February after an episcopate of forty-four years not at Hereford but at Bosbury, one of the twenty-four manors belonging to the bishopric of Hereford, and a favourite residence of its bishops. Blind and in failing health Athelstan had been assisted over the last fourteen years of his episcopate by Tremerin, bishop of St Davids, and he never recovered from the sack of Hereford. Edward the Confessor commissioned earl Harold to fortify Hereford against any similar raid in the future and the palace received an occupant of a quite different calibre from that of Athelstan.

His successor was Leofgar whose episcopate was to last but three months. A chaplain of earl Harold, despite his episcopal preferment, he refused to give up the secular habits he had followed as a priest. He offended the devout by declining to shave his moustache and when he 'abandoned his holy oil and his cross and spiritual weapons and took up his spear and sword'[7] and in company with the priests of the cathedral and the sheriff Aelfrith, he led an army against the Welsh.

Both Athelstan, described by his contemporaries as 'a man of great holiness' and his predecessor, bishop Athwulf, who came from Winchester, a minster which trained many bishops, were monks. Under them, despite their inevitable involvement in the political affairs of the border, the palace was a place of sanctity, learning and asceticism. Leofgar was a forerunner of a new kind of bishop who was also a feudal potentate, maintaining and leading his own army. For three months the palace walls re-echoed to talk of politics, war, and revenge against Gruffydd ap Llywellyn, though the disapproval generated by his conduct shows that this kind of episcopal activity was still a novelty. It is thought on the grounds of Leofgar's military stance and the fact that when he and his army encountered Gruffydd in battle on June 16th, 1056 it was in the valley of Machawy, some distance above Glasbury in present day southern Powys, it was he rather than Gruffydd who had taken the initiative. The result, however, was another brilliant victory for Gruffydd ap Llywelyn, and both bishop and sheriff were amongst the slain. It was four years before the palace was again occupied by a bishop of Hereford, the diocese in the meanwhile being administered by Ealdred, bishop of Worcester.

II. THE NORMAN BISHOPS AND THEIR PALACE

Leofgar's eventual successor as bishop of Hereford was Walter of Lorraine. Elected in 1060, it was not long before he, too, discovered the hazards of having one's cathedral and palace within the shadow of the castle. For in 1067 the castle was attacked by Bleddyn ap Cynfyn, prince of Powys, and his brother Rhiwallon who joined Eadric the Wild, a Mercian landowner with broad estates on the Welsh border. Walter of Lorraine died in 1079 and was succeeded by the versatile and scholarly Robert Losinga who also hailed from Lorraine. Before attempting the reconstruction of Athelstan's cathedral, still languishing from Gruffydd ap Llywelyn's desecration, Robert Losinga built for himself a handsome two-storeyed double chapel of a type common in Germany and northern France and based on Charlemagne's ninth century design at Aachen and with which he would have been familiar. Despite the protests of the Society of Antiquaries, it was demolished in 1737 by Henry Egerton, bishop of Hereford 1724-46, at the cost of fifty pounds when, apparently, it could have been restored for twenty. It was probably during Losinga's episcopate that Bishop's Castle was built to defend the bishop's estates there against the Welsh, its foundation being dated between 1085 and 1100.

Two of the original arches of this demolished chapel were incorporated into the wall of the cathedral's south cloister and are still to be seen in the palace garden. The nineteenth century antiquary J. Britton related in 1836 that the chapel's Norman arched entrance had 'at least ten receded mouldings, sprung from as many columns on each side.'[8] It was obviously built for use in conjunction with the bishop's palace as part of a proposed grand scheme of reconstruction, which was never completed, in which after the style of Durham and Canterbury, the palace would adjoin with its main rooms at first floor level. Perhaps Robert Losinga's energies and resources were exhausted by rebuilding the cathedral in the new Norman fashion at the same time. His new cathedral was not only in a new style, it was on a new site which overlay the town's central west-east thoroughfare, commemorated today by King Street and Castle Street, and was to the north of its Saxon predecessor.

Half a century later, in the episcopate of Robert de Bethune, 1131-48, the palace, rebuilt or not, was of sufficient dimensions for him to be able to offer its hospitality and the use of the chapel to forty monks from Llanthony abbey, consecrated in 1108, in the wildest part of the valley of the Honddu in the Black Mountains. Its founders joined the order of Augustinian canons and Robert de Bethune became its second prior. A true recluse by nature, it was with the greatest reluctance that he accepted preferment as bishop of Hereford and his biographer and companion, William of Wycombe, tells how when the time came for him to leave Llanthony 'it seemed to him that, like Adam of old, he was being driven from Paradise into exile.' His exile in Hereford was no doubt relieved by the companionship for two years of the monks of Llanthony who found themselves no longer able to endure the asperities of the Black Mountains. In 1138 they were transferred from de Bethune's palace to Llanthony Secunda, founded in the gentler climate of Gloucester.

The monks of Llanthony had hardly left the palace for their new home when once again the castle was beseiged in the course of the struggle between Stephen, grandson of William the Conqueror, and his cousin the Empress Matilda for the throne. Stephen celebrated his capture of Hereford castle by attending mass in the cathedral on Whitsunday 1138. But his triumph was short-lived. Miles, constable of Gloucester, having deserted Stephen for Matilda's side attacked Hereford in 1139 and took possession of the cathedral. Its clergy were expelled, the tower was used to fire from against the castle, and the nave became stabling. Robert de Bethune excommunicated Miles, now earl of Hereford, abandoned the palace and retired to Shobdon priory. Miles, however, had enjoyed his earldom but two years when he was accidentally shot by a companion while hunting in the Forest of Dean. Thus in due course Robert de Bethune was able to reconsecrate the cathedral, level the military defences, recall the clergy, restore its services, and repair the palace.

Robert de Bethune died at Châlons in 1148 and the Welsh *Chronicle of the Princes* recorded his death as that of 'a man who was, according to our judgement, pious and full of works and charity and a kind provider for the poor and an eminent ornament of the Church.' He was succeeded in turn by Gilbert Foliot, 1148-63, and Robert de Melun, 1163-67, after whom there was a six year interregnum during which in 1172 Hereford was ravaged by Iorwerth ap Owain, prince of

Gwynllwg, in revenge for the murder of his son by men of the earl of Gloucester from Cardiff. 'And after he had been slain, then his father and Hywel, his brother, and many others, because of that in no way trusting the king, ravaged the king's territory as far as Hereford and Gloucester, slaying, and burning and plundering without mercy.'[9]

The interregnum was brought to an end in the following year by the appointment of Robert Foliot, 1173-86, but it was during the episcopate of his successor, William de Vere, 1186-99, that the palace which does not make a show acquired the form, now concealed behind its modest façades, which has long been recognised as being that of one of the most important medieval secular structures remaining in England and the grandest of the surviving handful of the nation's pre-1200 timber buildings.

Courtly, sophisticated, and a lavish host, William de Vere came to Hereford familiar with recent architectural fashion and achievement as manifested in the palaces of Henry II, as well as in those of his fellow bishops, besides numerous clerestoried abbeys and cathedrals. From 1177-84 he had supervised Henry II's grandiose building project at Waltham Abbey and his epitaph proclaims that he 'built many noble buildings.'[10] He had come now to a border diocese which at this time enjoyed both status and wealth and was going to have an enlarged cathedral and for his household a palace of appropriate grandeur. The western boundary of his diocese ran with that of the Welsh see of St Davids, whose bishop, Peter de Leia, had been busily rebuilding his cathedral since 1180 and the work was still in progress. Moreover, he was familiar with the metropolitical ambitions of the bishops of St Davids and needed to assert the prestige of his own diocese to check any unhealthy Welsh territorial ambitions which could only be fulfilled at its expense. Thus, he enlarged Robert Losinga's cathedral by transforming its east end. This was achieved by demolishing its original three apses, erecting in their place two transepts and an ante-chapel to the Lady Chapel which was not built until the next century.

William de Vere's scheme for the palace was centred upon three large free-standing buildings: Robert Losinga's double chapel, a new hall, and a new separate chamber block. The dominating feature was the hall, one hundred and ten feet long and fifty-five feet wide. It was ecclesiastical in design with a nave from which its aisles were separated on both sides by four bays, of which three still survive in a fragmentary state. It was not built, however, of stone, but of Herefordshire

Surviving wall of Robert Losinga's 11th century double chapel in the palace garden.

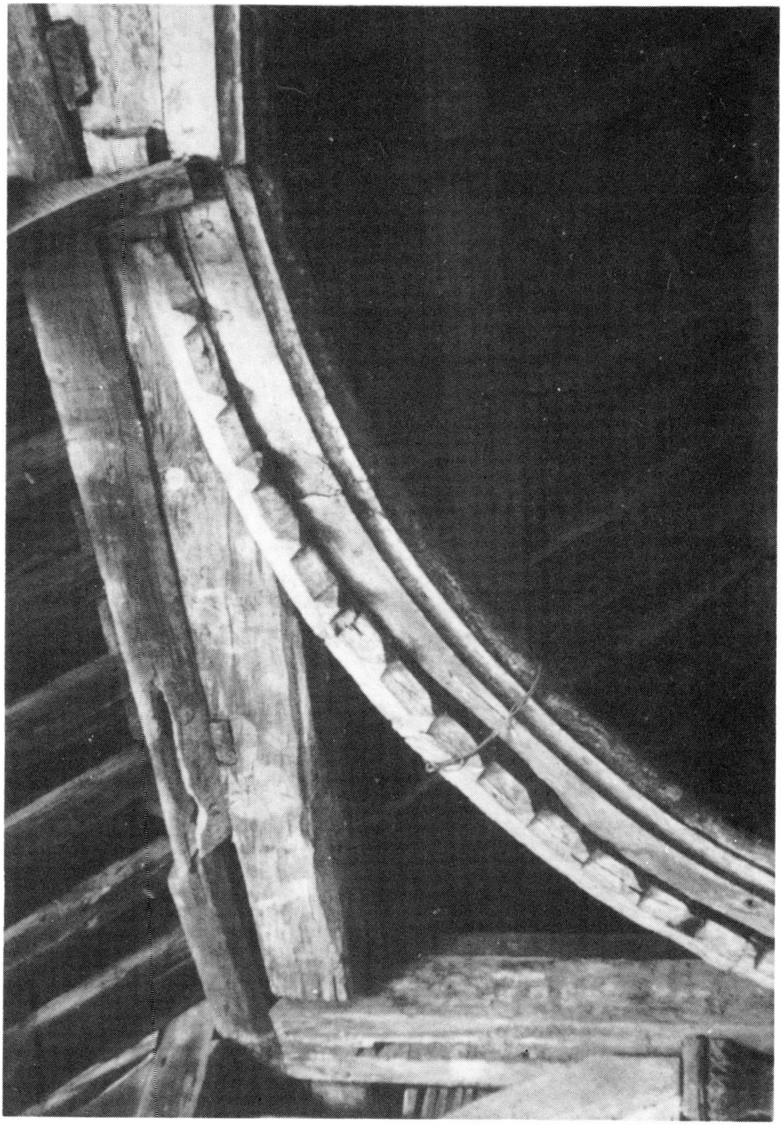

Timbers from William de Vere's medieval palace.

oak, and its timber pillars are two and a half feet square. The mouldings on the surviving arches have stone parallels in the north transept of Abbey Dore which was also built in the late 1180s. Their ornamentation was in the grand manner and traces of painted decoration can, in places, still be seen. 'Colour doubtless covered the whole of the plane surfaces as well as the woodwork and one cannot exclude the possibility that there was a coffered and painted ceiling, a fitting counterpart to the great painted ceiling of this date in Peterborough cathedral.'[11] Two half arches belonging to the hall's timber arcade have been preserved on either side of the archway of the palace gatehouse.

In 1841 bishop Musgrave in the course of his re-ordering of the palace built the present Romanesque porch to the hall to replace a predecessor of similar design which seems to have been the sole survivor of the external stonework of William de Vere's hall. The halls of Old Sarum and Canterbury had porches in a similar position, near the centre of a side wall.[12]

Some see it as essentially a conservative building, the last of a line of imposing clerestoried timber halls, whilst others argue that it reflects the latest developments in stone architecture at the end of the twelfth century. In his recent study of the palace, John Blair maintained that of the former opinion 'in so courtly a milieu this is scarcely convincing... Architecturally, it is thoroughly up to date for the 1190s. In its planning, it marks an important stage in the transition from the typical twelfth century manor-house, compartmentalized into separate buildings, to the standard late medieval plan with hall, chambers, and services integrated under one roof.'[13]

At the south, riverside, end of the hall there was a subsidary chamber-block on three floors over a basement which was below ground level on three sides. The ground floor was occupied by service rooms, but the block was too narrow to contain a grand chamber on the floors above and, instead, smaller chambers offered additional accommodation for what must have been a very large episcopal household for the Norman bishops of Hereford were Marcher Lords as well as diocesan bishops.

The third constituent of William de Vere's scheme was a detached chamber block, containing the bishop's great chamber on its first floor. Blair considers it would be surprising if Hereford did not have one of the stone chambers which were standard elements in bishops' palaces, and indeed in all aristocratic houses, of the late twelfth century. The site of this chamber block is suggested by a 1757 map of Hereford which shows in the plan of the palace a large building, aligned like the hall, north to south, and a little to the east of it and linked to it by a passage. This building was probably demolished in 1798 when the west, hall, end of the passage was rebuilt as a chapel.[14]

It is postulated that in the late twelfth century Broad Street continued in its southern course to the Wye at Palace Ford, not yet being diverted by the later palace gatehouse and prison. This earlier road-pattern may have influenced the lay-out of William de Vere's palace complex. Both Robert Losinga's chapel and the new hall both faced west to this road, across an outer court. The gap between the two buildings led to an inner court, closed on its eastern side by the new chamber-block.

Giraldus Cambrensis, archdeacon of Brecon and would-be bishop of St Davids stayed at the old palace in 1186, just after William de Vere's arrival at Hereford, with archbishop Baldwin and Ranulph de Glanvill, Henry II's justiciar, and their visit illustrates one of the functions of a Norman bishop's palace. The purpose of the meeting was to negotiate on Henry II's behalf with the Lord Rhys, the princely overlord of south Wales and Giraldus's uncle. Prebendary Moir saw it as yet another ambition of William de Vere to gather round him at Hereford a band of distinguished canons, of whom Giraldus was to be one. Perhaps it was on this occasion that the bishop saw that this ambitious and talented young man, still in his twenties, had much to offer Hereford.

Two years later, in March 1188, Giraldus, archbishop Baldwin, and Glanvill were back in Hereford when work on the new palace was well in hand. Their purpose was again as much political as religious. Archbishop Baldwin was about to begin his great journey through Wales, which Giraldus recorded in his famous *Itinerary,* ostensibly to preach the cause of the Third Crusade. Welsh soldiers were renowned for their competence which Henry II hoped would now be used against the Saracen rather than himself. Also, by celebrating mass at the high altar of each of the four Welsh cathedrals it was Baldwin's intention to assert his authority over the Welsh bishops who hankered, like Giraldus, after a national church independant of the rule of Canterbury, just as the Welsh princes strove for their independence of the English crown. Once again Ranulph de Glanvill was at Hereford on his way to further political discussions with the Lord Rhys next day at New Radnor.

The political role of the palace as the court of a Marcher Lord is again illustrated by the episcopate of Giles de Braose, 1200-15, William de Vere's successor. The second son of William de Braose, Lord of Brycheiniog, like most of the bishops when the whole country was excommunicated 1208-1214 in consequence of the conflict between King John and the pope, he went into exile on the Continent. On his return in 1213 he took his place in the royal counsels, but had not forgotten the past which included persecution, the death of his father in poverty abroad and of his mother and eldest brother in Windsor castle. Moreover, King John tarried in restoring to him the de Braose lands he had confiscated so that by 1215 'the bishop's heart was ripe for rebellion' and the palace became the headquarters of a military campaign for their retrieval.

First he sent his brother Reginald, a son-in-law of Llywelyn the Great, to Brycheiniog where we are told the leading men received him honourably 'and after that, Giles too came himself to Brycheiniog and gained possession of Brecon, and Radnor and Hay and Blaenllynfi and the castle of Builth without any resistance.'[15] By the autumn, however, he felt obliged to yield his obedience to the king with whom he made his peace on 21st October. But on his way back to Hereford he fell ill at Gloucester and died. A year later King John 'came to Hereford, and many armed men along with him. And he summoned to him Reginald de Braose and the princes of Wales to ask them to make a pact with him and to make peace. And since it availed him naught, he made for Hay and Radnor and burned the towns and destroyed the castles.'[16] Giles de Braose's successor was Hugh Foliot, 1219-1234, archdeacon of Salop, whom King John had nominated to the vacant see of St Davids in 1215, but had failed to secure his election.

III. THE MEDIEVAL BISHOPS AND THEIR PALACE

The Middle Ages, occupying for the present purpose the period from 1200-1500, saw the evolution of the bishops of Hereford from Marcher Lords to Prelate Princes who were statesmen and important national figures to the enhancement of the status of the palace. So it was that an occupant of the palace in this period might also be a Lord Chancellor or Treasurer of England, Chancellor of the University of Oxford, Chancellor of Ireland, Keeper of the King's Wardrobe, an ambassador, or royal chaplain and confessor. He would also have seen the effects of the Black Death and the Wars of the Roses upon his diocese. It was also the case that the demands of state upon the bishop meant he was often absent from his palace. Not all of the palace's occupants in this period were statesmen, of course: many were devout and scholarly and one was belatedly canonized. Moreover, the diocese of Hereford being part of the universal Church, some of those who came to occupy the see and lived in the palace could speak neither English nor Welsh.

The palace, of course, was not the only bishop's house in what was an extensive diocese in which travel was often both difficult and dangerous. These were occasions then when he would stay at one or other of the episcopal manors which at one time numbered as many as twenty-four and were scattered over the diocese and beyond at Ross, Upton Bishop, Ledbury, Eastnor, Bosbury, Colwall, Cradley, Bishop's Frome, Bromyard, Whitbourne, Grendon Bishop, Eaton Bishop, Hampton Bishop, Shelwick, Tupsley, and Stretton Sugwas where Sugwas Court, built in 1792 stands on the foundation of an earlier bishop's house. All that now remains of it is a Norman archway, now incorporated into the stables, but which originally belonged to a range of buildings probably containing the chapel whose front had traceried windows. During his short episcopate, 1234-1239, Ralph Maidstone, acquired a London house as the bishop's official residence there. Situated in the middle of the west side of old Fish Street, which led to London Bridge, it cost £140 and was called Monthalt House after the family that previously owned it. Its Hereford connection, however began in the previous century and in 1166 the castle of *Munhalt* is listed as belonging to the bishops of Hereford, presumably on lease. The manors of Sevenhampton and Prestbury, on the outskirts of modern Cheltenham near the racecourse, were beyond the diocesan boundaries in Gloucestershire and Goldhill was in Dorset, seven miles south of Shaftesbury. The bishop's manors were also a source of episcopal revenue and places of safety at times when civil commotions or epidemics made town living dangerous and unhealthy. Ross, for example, is classified in the *Pipe Rolls* as a defended house, Prestbury in its place-name commemorates the fortified place of the priest, and whilst it was possibly in the possession of the bishops of Hereford as early as 803, it was certainly theirs by the time of Edward the Confessor, and in 1209 'the Bishop had here a handsome stone house moated about.' The significance of the name of Bishop's Castle is self-explanatory.

The palace, however, at Hereford was unfortified and relied on the protection of the city walls and the castle which, as Peter D'Aigueblanche, 1240-68, discovered was not always adequate. He was archdeacon of Salop before becoming bishop of Hereford, but he came from Savoy and was rewarded with the bishopric by Henry III for his useful financial services to the state. He established his nephew John D'Aigueblanche as dean and welcomed both relatives and fellow countrymen to the diocese with preferment. The violence of the times, even within a bishop's palace, is illustrated by the murder of Bernard, prior of the French monastic house of Champagne, whilst saying mass there in the palace chapel during one of Peter D'Aigueblanche's absences abroad.

The bishop had returned by 1262 when Llywelyn ap Gruffydd, grandson of Llywelyn the Great, ravaged the Herefordshire lowlands as far as Weobley and Eardisley. This caused Peter D'Aigueblanche as a royal partizan to panic for his safety and he betook himself to Gloucester. Henry III had himself just returned from France and was in feeble health, but he was not impressed by the absence of the bishop and his clergy from their cathedral when he came to Hereford to organise his forces for a Welsh campaign. Threatened with Henry's anger and the loss of their stipends, Peter D'Aigueblanche and his clergy returned to Hereford only to be attacked and captured by a coalition of barons under Roger Clifford who removed him and his Savoyard canons to the Clifford castle at Eardisley. He was imprisoned there for three months, but was eventually paid 300 marks in compensation. Any enthusiasm he had for life in the palace at

Hereford had disappeared by now and he went to his manor at Stretton Sugwas where he died on November 27th 1268, having made his will the day before.[17]

The most saintly occupant of the palace and one who has appealed most to the popular imagination over the centuries, was probably Thomas Cantilupe, 1275-82, Peter D'Aigueblanche's successor but one. An aristocrat, connected with the de Braose and Pembroke families, and educated by his uncle Walter Cantilupe, bishop of Worcester, and Robert Kilwarby, archbishop of Canterbury, before becoming a graduate of the universities of Oxford and Paris, he went on to become chancellor of Oxford and chancellor of England, as well as archdeacon of Stafford, canon of York and London, and prebendary of Lichfield and Hereford.

In him the palace acquired a tenant of great spiritual devotion, who endured the constant discomfort of a hair shirt as part of his discipline of piety and penitence. But he could also be strong and intransigent, especially in the maintenance of his episcopal dignity and privileges. Thus he strenuously resisted the dimunition of his property thereabouts by the earl of Gloucester's claims to hunting rights on the Malvern hills and himself disciplined with a rod the cattle raiding lord of Clifford whom he compelled in penitence to walk barefoot to the cathedral's high altar. At the end of his life Thomas Cantilupe was himself excommunicated in a legal dispute with archbishop Pecham of Canterbury. Eventually he appealed successfully to pope Martin IV at Rome, but became ill on the return journey and died in Tuscany on 25th August 1282.

His bones were brought back and buried in his cathedral at Hereford in the Lady Chapel. Pilgrims came in their thousands to his shrine, which in 1287 was established in its present position in the cathedral's north transept, returning home with stories of miraculous cures. Royalty came, and bishops. So did money in thank-offerings and twice Edward I sent his falcons for a cure. Consequently it became the accepted wisdom that Thomas Cantilupe was a saint and Richard Swinfield, once his chaplain, now his successor, and always his ardent admirer, appealed to the pope for his canonization. A papal commission, which included the bishop of London and six lawyers, was sent to Hereford in 1307 to investigate Thomas Cantilupe's candidature for this honour. It stayed at the palace for several months, examining witnesses in the bishop's chapel of St Katherine and making an inventory of offerings at Cantilupe's shrine. Thirteen years later, in

1322, he was canonized. To honour him the bishops of Hereford changed their arms from the three crowns of the kings of East Anglia, which were those of king Ethelbert, the martyr patron of the cathedral. The new arms, which can be seen in the present great hall of the palace, are a rebus, or heraldic pun, on the name Cantilupe, three leopards' heads reversed and pierced by three fleurs-de-lys.

The domestic register of Richard Swinfield, 1282-1317, Thomas Cantilupe's successor, contains a record of the bishop's household at this time. It is a list of forty names; squires, serving-men, lesser servants, and thirteen pages. It names amongst others Ralph, clerk of the bishop's chapel, who was paid six shillings and eight pence a year for his services, John and Robert, carters; Ywenetto, larderer; Adam Harpin, falconer; William, door keeper; Thomas, palfreyman; and Robilardo the butler. The lifestyle of a bishop's palace at this time is reflected in a record of bulk buying by the steward of the bishop of Winchester: 118 flitches of bacon; 27 cheeses; 70 hens; and 29,130 herrings. Richard Swinefield died, however, not in his palace at Hereford, but in his espiscopal manor at Bosbury, in March 1316.

It was now the turn of a local man to live in the palace, for though he was 'considered the most powerful prelate of the province, saving the dignity of the archbishopric' Adam Orleton, 1317-27, took his name from a village in north-east Herefordshire. It belonged to the Mortimers, so powerful at Wigmore and Ludlow, with whom he sided against Edward II who, not unreasonably, accused him of treachery. He did, indeed, act as Queen Isabella's confidential adviser and supported her in her fanatical hatred of her husband whilst being aware of her infatuation with Roger Mortimer. He entertained her in the palace in October 1326 and it was from here that he set out to meet the king at Monmouth to demand the surrender of the Great Seal, returning six days later to conspire with Isabella for her husband's deposition. It was here, too, that in the following November she received the news that Edward II had been captured with his favourite, Hugh Despenser, and his chancellor Baldcock, the former to die, crowned with nettles, on a gallows fifty feet high in the city, the latter to be thrown into the bishop's prison which was within the palace grounds.[18]

It was through Orelton's influence that John Trilleck was elected bishop in 1344. Another man with local connections, his family came from Trelleck near Monmouth and it was during his episcopate that the Black Death which reached England in 1348, swept into Herefordshire the following year. Forty-six per cent of the diocese clergy succumbed to the epidemic with which it is probably not unconnected that in 1350 the body of St Thomas Cantilupe was moved from the transept back to the Lady Chapel in the presence of Edward III, bishops, and noblemen. Tradition has it that the shrine was also carried in procession through the city to avert the plague. At a rather more trivial level it is related that during John Trilleck's episcopate a citizen of the city entered his palace and carried off the porter to the city gaol and took away the keys of the palace 'to the great inconvenience of the bishop.' What accommodation was offered by the palace at this period is uncertain, but it must have compared favourably with that of the episcopal residence at Prestbury for which a 1344 list of dilapidations mentions the stable, oxhouse, great stable, pigstye, cowhouse, three barns, an old chamber within the inner gateway, dairy, granary, chamber of the squires and clerks, hall, which being forty feet by fifty was of palatial proportions, kitchen, larder, brewhouse, middle-chamber, chapel, cellar, and lord's chamber. In 1356, during Trilleck's episcopate, the cathedral chapter agreed to reduce the number of the bishop's manor houses to six, keeping besides the palace at Hereford, only the houses at Bishop's Castle, Bosbury, London, Prestbury, Sugwas, and Whitbourne.

The survival of the Welsh language in western Herefordshire and southern Shropshire and the sizable Welsh element in their population meant that Welsh was one of the languages often heard in the palace. There was also an intermittent succession of bishops at Hereford who had either been translated from or to a Welsh diocese. For some translation offered welcome escape from a Snowdonian Siberia and greater proximity to London, the centre of things, and for all it offered a better stipend. One of the earliest occupants of the palace to have been translated from a Welsh diocese was John Gilbert, 1375-89, who came to Hereford from Bangor. Walsingham considered this renowned scholar and administrator, who was once a Dominican friar, 'more eloquent than trustworthy', but he enjoyed the confidence of the Black Prince for whom he was confessor and the executor of his will. He was also a papal auditor and was deemed useful in his services to both king and pope. In 1389 he returned to Wales as bishop of St Davids, attracted perhaps by an enhanced income. One suspects whilst he was bishop of Hereford he spent more time in his London house than in the palace at Hereford. Such a house was essential for a man of affairs like John Gilbert and whilst at Bangor he had sought and obtained full legal title to Bangor House in London's Shoe

Lane. But whether he lived in London or Hereford it is certain that both palace and diocese were well within the compass of state affairs and papal politics, for in 1389 Richard II had wanted his secretary Richard Medford to be elected as bishop of St Davids and it was on the insistence of Urban VI that John Gilbert instead was translated there from Hereford. A weak king had to yield to a strong pope.

Some bishops preferred to live outside the city in one of the episcopal manors to the palace. These houses did not entirely lack the comforts or the sophistication of their palatial counterpart in Hereford. Thus, Edmund Lacy, 1417-20, left his successor but one Thomas Spofford, 1422-48,[19] a pair of organs which he had installed in the manor at Whitbourne. Thomas Spofford who spent much of his personal wealth on the cathedral fabric also improved the manor at Stretton Sugwas, where he set up a window in its chapel which is now in Ross on Wye parish church, besides probably completing the bishop's cloister from the cathedral to the palace, adding thereby to the latter's convenience.

The final recorded incident of significance to occur in the medieval period of the palace's history took place in 1461 during the episcopate of John Stanbury, 1453-74,[20] who was another bishop of Hereford translated from Bangor. A Cornishman, so he was not unfamiliar with the Celtic fringe which still includes western Herefordshire in its embrace. At Bangor his generosity helped the restoration of the cathedral recovering from the ravages of the rebellion of Owain Glyndwr and at Hereford he is remembered for building the cloistered accommodation of the vicars choral. It was during his time that after the battle of Mortimer's Cross in 1461 which established Edward Mortimer as Edward IV the new king received homage at the palace, though he was not formally proclaimed king until his arrival in London, a few weeks later.[21]

IV. THE REFORMATION

The sixteenth and seventeenth centuries were as much a time of change and innovation for the palace as they were for the cathedral nearby. The last pre-Reformation bishop of Hereford was Charles Booth, 1516-35, who was previously archdeacon of Buckingham. His episcopal predecessors had been Marcher Lords, with heavy military responsibilities for the defence of the Marches, but Charles Booth had a more political role and was chancellor of the Council of the Marches which met at Ludlow castle. With lavish magnificence he extended the north porch of the cathedral which had been begun by his predecessor, Richard Mayew, 1504-16, superimposing a chapel upon it. He constructed his own tomb with his effigy, and the coffin, too. In his will he left his library to the cathedral, a Netherlands tapestry for the altar, a ring for the shrine of St Thomas Cantilupe, and 'a good dinner for the ministry and for the mayor and townsmen, ten fat oxen, thirty fat sheep, ten calves, etc., if funds permit.'

Charles Booth made considerable alterations to the palace which involved diverting the main road south from the city across the Wye bridge. Though a bridge existed here by the early twelfth century, it is postulated that Broad Street and Palace Ford formed the north-south axis of the Saxon burgh,[22] and it was alongside this road that William de Vere's palace was built. Booth's alterations involved building the palace's northern range to accommodate its new kitchens. Their north face is still timber-framed, though the south face was later cased in the mellow brick which so enhances the appearance of these buildings. One of its original bracket windows, a local variant for Oriel windows, remains. Across the path of the former main road he erected the present Tudor gateway with its timber framed gable above, and massive wooden door with two chamfered archways below. Most of the rooms inside this range have their original moulded and chamfered ceiling beams. Neither carved date nor inscription record Charles Booth as the instigator of these improvements, but in 1645 Richard Symonds found the bishop's arms 'often upon the walls of the palace', no doubt recording his innovations. Their effect seems to have been to have made the palace the most comfortable residence in the vicinity of Hereford for when commissioners were appointed in 1535 on his death to administer the temporalities of the diocese on behalf of Henry VIII, they wrote to ask that if they were ever re-appointed for a similar task 'we may have the liberty to lie in the bishop's palace ... as no other place is so suitable.' Charles Booth also did work on Monthalt House and the fact he died at Whitbourne Manor suggests that he may have made improvements there as well.

On May 14th, 1553, Charles Booth appointed a certain Thomas Belamye as his porter, and speaks of 'the house rebuilt by us and assigned by us to the same office.' The holder of this office had charge of all the canons' houses and installed their occupants. He was also keeper of the bishop's prison which stood in the south west corner of the forecourt and was one of three such establishments in different parts of the diocese for the accommodation of those incarcerated by the bishop's court. The keeper had to find nine securities of £40 apiece against the escape of any of his prisoners.

The effect of the Reformation on the palace was domestic rather than doctrinal, a bachelor establishment changing into married quarters, since bishops were now free to marry and make the palace a home for both themselves and their families. The break with Rome also meant that those who now lived in the palace were always the king's subjects and no longer came from continental Europe and as was the case of Peter D'Aigueblanche totally unfamiliar with the language of their flock.

The early post-Reformation bishops of Hereford seem to have been too taken up with ecclesiastical projects and theological propaganda to bother about either their Hereford or London homes and John Skipp, 1539-1552, granted Lord Clinton a lease of Monthalt House at a shilling a year for 200 years. This was annulled later by Queen Mary and the house reverted to the see. John Skip died there and was in fact buried in the chapel at Monthalt. His successor but one was Robert Parfew,[23] alias Wharton, 1554-1557, another translation from Wales where he was bishop of St Asaph for eighteen years. It was perhaps fortunate for diocese and palace alike that his stay at Hereford lasted only three years for at St Asaph he granted away rights of next presentation to forty of the one hundred and fifty livings in the diocese and many of them to people whose names suggest they were his relatives and strangers to St Asaph. The palace, however, may not have been to his taste, for two years later the staunchly protestant John Scory,

1559-85, arrived in Hereford and found it an 'uncommodious and unwholesome dwelling'. He therefore proposed to pull down part of it and reconstruct the rest. Having made his plans with the carpenters and masons and prepared the timbers for the work he sought the cathedral chapter's permission for it to proceed. But the chapter, offended no doubt by his denunciation of what he considered to be 'the blasphemy, pride, ignorance, and superstition' of their cathedral, deferred making any decision on the grounds that a matter of such importance needed the presence of all its members which would be difficult to achieve. Consequently prevarication and procrastination won the day and the project was abandoned.

Having a bishop's wife now in the palace also brought a new dimension to diocesan politics. John Scory's son was made a prebendary and the bishop's wife held three prebendal portions in Bromyard, to the resentment of the cathedral chapter. The financial rewards of this arrangement were more than off balanced by the bishop's less successful dealings with Elizabeth I who persuaded him to surrender Bishop's Castle in Shropshire, Prestbury in Gloucestershire, as well as Ledbury and Ross, deemed to be the see's best manors, in exchange for some less profitable advowsons. He also surrendered Monthalt House, the chapel of which became a parish church. He died at his manor house at Whitbourne.

The palace appears to have appealed no more to John Scory's successor, Herbert Westphaling, 1586-1601, for he had an estate and residence at Mansel Gamage. It was, of course, a period of great change in domestic architecture when greater privacy and comfort were deemed essential and the basically medieval structure of the palace, based on an open hall, did not lend itself easily to redevelopment without very drastic change. Moreover, Westphaling was very sensitive to his own dignity in the matter of episcopal accommodation. He complained to the executors of bishop Scory that in his time the house at Bosbury had been much destroyed and all that had happened since was that an addition had been made to what was left of the building, whereby though it was now 'fit for a good knight, or gentleman, it was short for a bishop.' His portrait, painted on a wooden panel, now hangs in the conference room and is the earliest in the palace's collection of episcopal portraits.

V. THE PALACE DURING THE COMMONWEALTH

The Reformation not only meant married bishops and their wives in the palace, but also their children. One would have expected this to have meant further modifications at this time to the internal arrangements of the palace to provide nurseries, play rooms, and additional bedrooms. But it is uncertain whether this was actually the case. There is little doubt that the priests' houses in the diocese were suitably enlarged for family living, but little was done to the bishop's numerous manor houses to acknowledge the advent of married bishops. Only Bosbury was added to by a bishop in the sixteenth century, John Scory. Whitbourne, which from the fourteenth century was the most popular of the episcopal manors and remained in use until the time of bishop Bisse who died in 1721, dates in its present form from late fifteenth century. It was beloved of the scholarly and versatile Francis Godwin, 1617-33, but appears to have had little done to it until it was occupied by the Birch family who made additions to it c.1670-80. It is thought that the palace itself had to wait until Philip Bisse rebuilt it in early Georgian times.

The seventeenth century began at Hereford with the tennis playing Robert Bennett, 1603-17, who came to the palace from the deanery of Windsor. He spent considerable sums of money in the restoration of his episcopal properties and commemorated his tenure of them with carvings of his name and coat of arms, a cross between demi-lions rampant which can be seen in the palace in an enriched cartouche of stained glass inserted over a garden door. His successor, Francis Godwin, 1617-33, had little taste for the palace and preferred to live at Whitbourne where he could write undisturbed by the distractions of episcopal affairs. His *Catalogue of the Bishops of England* won him the approval of Elizabeth I and the bishopric of Llandaff. The judicious dedication of the second edition to James I secured his preferment to Hereford. He died at Whitbourne and was buried there. His portrait hangs in the great hall of the palace and is a copy of one at Christ Church, Oxford given by Lord Saye and Sele who commissioned William Smith in 1874 to make it.

Francis Godwin's effective successor[24] was Augustine Lindsell, 1634, a classical scholar and antiquary, who was translated to Hereford from Peterborough, and who both lived and died in the palace. Sadly his episcopate had lasted but a year when he was found dead in the palace library. The original inscription on his tomb in the south-east transept of the cathedral ascribed his death to gall stones. The episcopate of his successor, Matthew Wren, was even shorter. Another dean of Windsor, he remained only a few months at Hereford en route for the bishoprics of Norwich and Ely. One of his kinsmen, however, was Christopher Wren which has led to the speculation as to what *might* have happened architecturally to the palace had the bishop remained at Hereford longer.

The ineffectual Thomas Field, who followed Matthew Wren, like Francis Godwin, also came from Llandaff, though via St Davids, and had six children. By pleading poverty on their account to the Duke of Buckingham he secured the see of Llandaff only to find it had little with which to enhance his financial position. So he suggested to the duke that Hereford was what he really needed. St Davids, however, became vacant first and he went there for seven years before acquiring Hereford. But too late, and within six months he was dead.

Puritanism, which under Sir Robert Harley of Brampton Bryan had some strength in Herefordshire, had little sympathy for Anglican liturgy and order. Bishops and priests were regarded with particular disfavour and George Coke, 1636-46, 'a grave and studious man, well beloved in his diocese', was one of the ten bishops imprisoned in the Tower of London in 1641 on a charge of treason brought against them by the Puritan minded House of Commons. For eighteen weeks George Coke languished in prison and it was not long after his return to the palace that civil war broke out between Charles I and Parliament. This was in August 1642.

By the following September Hereford was beginning to know the meaning of civil war. Lord Stamford with a parliamentarian force was at the gates demanding admittance. The city, unwilling to receive him, was equally unable to resist him. In spite of its castle and city walls with their moat, sixteen towers, and gates, no defence had been organised. The castle was in decay; the gates ruinous. So Stamford found himself in possession of Hereford and made his quarters in the palace, whilst George Coke is said to have been watching events from his manor at Whitbourne.

Stamford's stay was short and finding he had insufficient forces with which to control the city he left for Gloucester in December 1642. For a few months Hereford was in royalist hands. But again the tide turned and in April 1643 Sir William Waller appeared with a parliamentarian army of 2,500 men from Gloucester. The city capitulated, but within a month the royalists were again in control and remained so until 1645 when Charles I was three times in Hereford. The first occasion was on 19th June when he stayed two days after his disastrous defeat at Naseby. He returned on 4th September, dining that day in the palace. He came again on 18th September for the last time, on his way to Presteign.

During July and August 1645 Hereford was besieged by 14,000 Scots presbyterians under Lord Leven. Those defending the city burned all the houses outside the walls, destroyed St Martin's church which then stood near the Wye and commanded the bridge and palace, and broke down one of the bridge's arches. But the siege was abandoned and on September 4th, 1645 Charles I entered Hereford in triumph. But the city's troubles for 1645 were not over and there was another siege in December. Under Colonel John Birch Hereford was captured by the parliamentarians. John Birch was appointed governor of the city and occupied part of the bishop's palace. Captain Silas Taylor, an antiquary and musician, had the other part. He possessed a chamber organ and somewhat in contradiction to the puritan spirit gave musical parties in the palace at which the composer Matthew Locke, a suspected papist, conducted the performers.

John Birch obtained possession of Whitbourne manor and, a shrewd business man, bought the bishop's palace for £11 and 'the materials in the said palace' for £48. In all he acquired the palace and the episcopal manors at Shelwich, Barton, Tupsley, Eaton Bishop, Hampton Bishop, and Stretton Sugwas for £2,475 2s 3d. The dispossessed George Coke retired to Eardisley where he died in December 1646.

VI. FROM THE RESTORATION TO THE NINETEENTH CENTURY

The restoration of the monarchy in the person of Charles II in 1660 besides leading to another of Hereford's short episcopates, this time that of Nicholas Monk who was bishop from January to December 1661, also saw the restoration of the Church of England and the Book of Common Prayer. Once again the bishop of Hereford lived in the palace. But what was regained at Hereford was lost in London, for the Great Fire of 1666 destroyed Monthalt House, the bishop's town house. Indeed the palace was now the only house of the bishops of Hereford since by now the episcopal manors had also disappeared. The role of bishops had changed and they were now less involved in affairs of state and more concerned with their cathedrals and dioceses. Consequently the palace became an administrative centre as well as a home. Structural alterations were necessary to adapt it to its new functions and these were carried out spasmodically as need arose. It is likely that they reflected the tastes and ideas of the bishop's wife as often as those of the bishop himself. The fact that bishops were now resident at Hereford more often also meant that the palace and bishop's study assumed greater importance, especially if the bishop was a scholar.

Herbert Croft, 1662-91, who had been a courageous opponent of puritan excess, moved from the deanery to the palace, where in 1675 he wrote his timely plea for tolerance, *The Naked truth: or, the true state of the primitive church.* His portrait, showing him as a benign, kindly man, hangs in the great hall. Though it is a copy, it is thought to be one of the best in the palace's collection of episcopal portraits.

During his episcopate, in 1662, the Hearth Tax was introduced whereby '...every dwelling and other house and edifice and all lodgings ... shall be chargeable ... for every fire hearth...'. The returns by which liabilities under the tax were assessed give historians a useful source of social information. The Herefordshire return for Lady Day 1664[25] reveals that the palace had twenty-eight hearths upon which the bishop had to pay fifty-six shillings tax a year. The same return shows that the deanery, from which Herbert Croft moved to the palace, was rated as having only eleven hearths, for which twenty-two shillings a year were payable. These statistics give us some idea as to the comparable size and relative comfort of deanery and palace at this time. One can imagine, too, the number of servants and the amount of fuel required to keep twenty-two open fires well stoked on a winter's day. On Lady Day 1664 the entire city of Hereford was assessed for 1,230 hearths a fact which, no doubt, at times made the bishop all the more appreciative of the smoke free zones he could enjoy away from Hereford in the vicinity of his manor houses.

Croft's successor but one,[26] Humphrey Humphries, 1701-2, translated from Bangor, was also a considerable scholar. Described in his day as 'the best Welshman living', he was a native of Meirionydd, and a master of the Welsh language which must have been heard frequently in the palace in his time because he maintained at Hereford his scholarly contacts and interests in both Welsh and Classical antiquities. His relations with the townsfolk of Hereford were less fruitful. One of his servants fell into the Wye near the palace and drowned. The matter might not have attracted public notice but for its legal implications, for in defiance of the bishop's rights the man was buried next day by order of the county coroner. Humphrey Humphries resented this as an infringement of his episcopal rights and protested, but to no effect.

Humphrey Humphries' successor, Philip Bisse, 1713-21, was also translated from a Welsh diocese, this time St Davids. It was in his episcopate that the most ambitious of the eighteenth century schemes of reconstruction were undertaken, though it was with some exaggeration that his monument in the cathedral recorded amongst his achievements 'the rebuilding of the palace practically from its foundations.'

Philip Bisse was full of architectural projects which included the panelling of the cathedral choir, 'at very great cost, but in a manner totally at variance with ancient or modern principles'[27] adding supports to the central tower, and rebuilding two canons' houses. His brother, Thomas Bisse, was chancellor of the cathedral and played an important part in the early days of the Three Choirs Festival, whereas he himself spent £3,000 of his own money on the reconstruction of the palace which he found old fashioned and inconvenient. The great hall was re-modelled and divided into five compartments. The new hall, which stretched across the building, rather than along it, was a fragment of the size of its Norman predecessor, but is basically the present great hall. In it arches sprang from giant Doric and Ionic pilasters and an entablature, hiding the original Norman timbers. A frieze, decorated predictably with crossed croziers, encompassed the room. The new central ceiling was flat, and the side aisles were also plastered, their ceiling being given apse ends. Amongst the other rooms created were a drawing room, which was left with an exposed Norman pier, and handsomely panelled,[28] a library, and a dining room. Above, extra bedrooms were provided for the large episcopal families of the period.

The exterior was clad in brick and stone, of which some of the latter was brought from the ruined chapter-house which had collapsed after the removal of its lead roof during the civil war. Isaac Taylor's 1757 map of Hereford shows the palace finished at the north wall of the present conference room and at the south end as it does at present. One of the map's marginal vignettes depicts it as having an eighteenth century sash windowed east front which was also probably part of Bisse's scheme. Part of it still survives today,[29] the large and handsome sash windows of the south end of the west front also belong to this period.

Prebendary Moir thought that the clue to Philip Bisse's ambitious architectural activities lay in his marriage with Bridget, daughter of the first duke of Leeds, who was also earl of Danby, marquess of Carmarthen, Treasurer of England, and a Knight of the Garter. Her first husband was Charles fitz Charles, earl of Plymouth and illegitimate son of Charles II. Philip Bisse was her chaplain and though he married the widowed Lady Bridget in 1704, the marriage was not publicly acknowledged until 1706. She died in 1718, aged 54, and was buried in the cathedral.

Philip Bisse left the bishops who succeeded him a palace the elegance of which was only equalled by its inconvenience. The walls of his rebuilt great hall were carried up to the main roof and cut the first floor of the palace into two distinct sections between which there was no means of communication. Likewise the palace has no central ceremonial staircase and a modest, rather narrow staircase at the south end of the house still has to serve to give access to the first floor. At this time the main entrance to the palace led into the great hall and the bishop's quarters through which visitors to the bishop's wife would also have to pass. The kitchen wing was at the opposite end of the house to the bishop's drawing room, dining room, and study. It is not surprising, perhaps, that a twentieth century architect should have thought 'the house is not compactly planned and lacks a good staircase while passages are rambling and are not too well lighted.'[30]

East front of the palace showing Bisse's alterations in the centre and the Victorian changes at either end.

Bisse's great hall before its restoration in 1975.

Philip Bisse's successor at Hereford was Benjamin Hoadly, 1721-23, a prominent ecclesiastical spiralist, who was translated from Bangor and the last of the Welsh episcopal translations. He was here for too short a time to make much impact on either the diocese or the palace, which despite its recent extensive renovation did not dispose him to tarry at Hereford longer than necessary, and after two years he moved on to Winchester via Salisbury. He was however a scholar whose writing opposed the prevalent sacerdotal high church thinking of his day. A broad churchman, it was his opinion that all that mattered in religion was sincerity, which caused William Law to complain that 'the bishop has left us neither priests, sacraments, nor Church.'

The improvements to the palace made by Philip Bisse which failed to commend Hereford to Benjamin Hoadly fell into decay during the lengthy episcopate of the aristocratic Henry Egerton, 1724-46. He was the fifth son of the earl of Bridgewater and came to Hereford from a canonry at Oxford. He was said to be, however, 'miserably covetous' and besides causing the destruction of Robert Losinga's double chapel, he was accused of 'allowing the palace and his parsonage at Whitbourne to go to ruin to the great damage of his successors.' One of these successors was the equally aristocratic Lord James Beauclerk, 1746-87, eighth son of the duke of St Albans and whose somewhat mediocre portrait hangs in the palace in an appropriately obscure passage. The original hangs in the hall at the Queen's College, Oxford.

Those who have a taste for scandal dwell upon the fact that Nell Gwynne, Charles II's mistress, was James Beauclerk's grandmother and that she was reputed to have been born in a cottage, now demolished but commemorated by a plaque, adjoining the wall of the palace's kitchen garden where once stood one of the bishop's prisons. No doubt, if there be any substance to the claim, she little imagined a grandson of hers would ever be a bishop living in the palace overlooking her old home. The bishop had frequent disagreements with the dean and chapter, one of which was over the right of way through the palace grounds to the chapter timber-yard. His tenancy of the palace is commemorated by the fireplace he inserted into the great hall, but the great architectural event of his episcopate was the dramatic collapse on Easter Monday, 1786 of the entire west end, including the west tower, of his cathedral.

The reconstruction of the west end of the cathedral took place during the episcopate of John Butler, 1788-1802. The task was entrusted to James Wyatt, a leading and versatile architect of the day. There were changes at the palace, too, and in 1798 the west end of the passage which once linked the medieval detached chamber block to the main palace building was converted into a chapel, leading out of Philip Bisse's new great hall. What had survived of the chamber block was probably demolished at this time. Its filled-in undercroft remains under the palace lawn awaiting excavation at some future date.[31]

It was at this time that John Price in his *Historical account of the City of Hereford,* 'embellished with elegant views' and published in 1796, wrote of Hereford's 'handsome Palace, near the west end of the Cathedral, from which there is a most delightful view of the Wye, Rotherwas Wood, Dynedor Camp, etc., being placed in a charming situation on the banks of the river. Though the fabric as appears by its structure, was modelled a great while ago, it has not withstanding many appartments furnished with much elegance. The gardens, which are extensive, are laid out upon a gentle declevity contiguous to the water, exposed to a fine southern aspect, and commanding the same happy prospects.'

One who expected to walk in those gardens in August 1802 was Lord Nelson who was then visiting Hereford, accompanied by Lady Hamilton and her husband. The crowd took the horses out of the carriage at the Wye bridge and drew it in triumph to the City Arms Hotel. Here Nelson received John Butler's apology for not coming to pay his respects to him owing to his age, he was then eighty-five, and infirmity aggravated by gout. After the official reception, however, it is said that Nelson left the duke of Norfolk and the company at the hotel and, as a son of a clergyman, went along Broad Street to the palace to call on the aged bishop. His portrait hangs in the palace's conference room and is well thought of as a work of art.

Prebendary Moir noted that in the nineteenth century, 'remote from the effect of the Napoleonic wars, the Reform Bill, Catholic Emancipation, or industry's dark satanic mills, Hereford preserved a Barchester-like air of serenity. The bishop could enjoy the secluded palace, the placid Wye, the calm of the cloisters and choral service.'[32] Enjoyment of the palace's seclusion was enhanced by re-ordering it according to current tastes and fashion and 'the building itself was much improved by Bishop Huntingford, also by Dr Musgrave, late of this see.'[33] Exactly what improvements were implemented by George Huntington, 1815-1832, is uncertain, but according to the *Cambrian Traveller's Guide* of 1813 the palace on the bishop's arrival at Hereford from Gloucester in 'its outward appearance was by no means prepossessing, tho' many of the apartments were fitted up with elegance.' It was Thomas Musgrave, 1837-47, however, who gave the palace its present predominantly Victorian aspect.

One suspects that on his arrival at Hereford Thomas Musgrave found the palace not only unprepossessing without, but also inelegant within, and was reluctant to live in it until it was rebuilt. Certainly neither he nor any member of his family was in residence for the 1841 census and the palace was run by two manservants, aged eighty and seventy, respectively with the assistance of a youth of twenty and three female servants, the youngest of which was a girl of fourteen. Interestingly, the only other occupant was a certain Joseph Hancocks, aged twenty, and whose occupation was given as being that of an architect. He was probably an articled assistant of Philip Hardwick, 1792-1870.

In 1842 Dean Merewether recalled how in the Autumn of 1840 he 'was walking with Mr Hardwick, the eminent Architect employed by the Bishop of the diocese, in preparing plans for the alterations contemplated at the palace.'[34] Philip Hardwick was indeed an eminent architect, better known for the monumental Euston Arch or Propylaeum he designed as a ceremonial gateway to the London terminus of the London and Birmingham Railway. His designs for 'the bishop's palace at Hereford with proposed alterations' were exhibited at the Royal Academy in 1840 and were, no doubt, not unconnected with his election as an RA in 1841. Hardwick's designs were first drawn up in 1833, soon after Thomas Musgrave's arrival at Hereford, and it is uncertain as to whether they were implemented in stages or they had to wait until 1841 to be completed in one go. A drain pipe bearing that date suggests that this latter suggestion was the case as does the survival of an 1841 contract for alterations to the palace. The improvements involved replacing the north bay of the original palace with the wing with which we are familiar nowadays as being occupied by the diocesan offices. The original romanesque porch and the sole survivor of the eleventh century stonework was restored 'in a praiseworthy manner' as the palace's principal entrance. The episcopal identity of the gargoyles which adorn both sides of the entrance is an interesting matter for speculation. The east front of the palace was also restyled and the stable block built on the western side of the palace forecourt.

Thomas Musgrave was translated to the archbishopric of York in 1847 and Hereford viewed the appointment of his successor, Renn Dickson Hampden, 1848-68, with dismay. The arms of both men attractively worked in stained glass and appropriately displayed in juxtaposition can be seen in the fan light above the french windows leading from the great hall to the palace gardens. Regius professor of Divinity at Oxford and a fellow of Oriel College Renn Hampden was an outstanding scholar intimate with the leaders of the Oxford Movement though he shared little of their theology. Hereford, however, thought his liberal views heretical and there was considerable opposition to his appointment which was thought to have been unnecessarily provocative. In the event, instead of being arrogant and aggressive as had been expected, he turned out to be shy and retiring, though his wife proved to be a formidable figure within the palace and beyond. They seemed to have lived quietly in the palace with, according to the Census returns of 1851 and 1861, a small staff which included, for the needs of the bishop's wife, a Swiss lady's maid.

Once again, however, changes were made to the fabric of the palace. Dr Hampden enlarged the drawing room, leading off from the south side of the great hall by amalgamating it with the adjoining library, 'a finely proportioned dome being made in the centre of the ceiling to correct its comparative want of height.'[35] This formed 'a spacious appartment with half a dozen windows opening into the Palace gardens.'[36] The form and scope of any other changes made at this time are unknown but a dated drain pipe records they occurred in 1862 and they may have included the introduction of piped gas to the palace. A guide book of 1867 describes the gas fittings in the cathedral which was then lit by 250 jets and one would expect the palace to have been piped for gas at the same time.

Great houses inevitably acquire myths and the bishop's palace at Hereford is no exception. Dr Hampden was succeeded by James Atlay, 1868-1895, whose arms depicted in vigorous stained glass, with those of Robert Bennet, can be seen in the fan light above a garden door at the south end of the palace. He came to Hereford from Leeds by way of Ripon where he was a canon residentiary. At Leeds parish church he followed the great Dr Hook as vicar and was himself, despite the undeserved strictures of Francis Kilvert that he was 'overbearing and imperious' a great pastoral bishop, anxious always to be accessible to his flock. Early in his episcopate he said 'If there is any person ... who may want at any time either my advice or my presence at a ceremony or whatever it may be, he has only to write and let me know, or what is better, come and see me at Hereford, and I will only be too happy to attend to his wishes at once.'[37] Perhaps for the more informal comfort of those who visited him at the palace its drawing-room was re-ordered, giving rise to the story that at Mrs Atlay's insistance the lower part of one of the original oak posts of the medieval hall was removed for appearance's sake. So great an authority as Pevsner relates, though with some hesitation, the offending bishop's wife to have been an anonymous twentieth century successor to Mrs Atlay.[38] In 1872 in a spectacular ceremony in the Shire Hall the bishop was presented with a new pastoral staff, the cost of which had been met by public subscription. The presentation was made by the earl of Powys whose brother, the Honourable George Herbert, was at that time dean of the cathedral. The wood of this new staff, which is over six feet tall, and whose elaborate design and bejewelled silver work is characteristic of its period, was taken from one of the surviving medieval oak pillars in the palace. Perhaps it came from the removed pillar in the new drawing room.

By now Philip Bisse's chapel leading from the great hall had been demolished and replaced by another chapel built on to the north end of the palace and looking on to the gardens. It was small and plain and is remembered by some for its murals which in more recent times it was deemed a kindness to have covered up. The household met here daily for family prayers. It is now a conference room. The gentlemen's smoking room was above the nearby dining room, which is now another conference room. It was far removed from the ladies of the house in the drawing room at the opposite end of the building. It is strange that the nursery was also at the north end of the palace and well away from the bishop's own quarters. James Atlay was an enthusiastic family man with eight children. The Census returns for 1881 record that the bishop, who was then 63 and his wife 41, lived in the palace with them, the youngest of whom was on the census day a seventeen day old unbaptized infant son. With so many children, ranging in age from a few days to a twenty year old undergraduate son, perhaps the bishop did not want to see too much of his children. Likewise it is perhaps a Freudian reflection of the cool relationship which sometimes existed between the bishop and the cathedral chapter in which they, too, did not want to see too much of each other, that most of the main rooms of the palace have either a southern or eastern aspect. There are no views of the cathedral from the house except from what was the long first floor passage of the kitchen wing.

The 1881 Census returns record, with careful differentiation and ranking, the resident palace staff as consisting of a governess, a cook, a lady's maid, two housemaids, a school room maid, a nursery maid, a kitchen maid, a scullery maid, two footmen, a coachman, and a gardener. The palace obviously had an economic as well as social importance to the city of Hereford as an important employer of labour.

James Atlay died in his bedroom in the palace on Christmas Eve 1894. There are two portraits of him: a copy of the 1893 presentation portrait by John Collier commemorating his twenty-five years as bishop hangs in the Conference Room. An earlier portrait of 1881 in oils by E. A. F. Pryane hangs, at least according to the 1976 Palace Inventory, in 'the Conference Room Cupboard.' His successor was John Percival who saw the palace move into the twentieth century with the acquisition of a telephone and introduction of electricity, the City of Hereford electricity supply having commenced operations in December 1899 and included the cathedral close and palace in its circuit. It was also at this time that the palace acquired a rudimentary secretariat, the predecessor of the present bishop's office with its three secretaries: the bishop's chaplain acted as his secretary and had his own office. 'In the centre are two large escritoires, a *typewriter* standing on one, and the other having all the accessories of penmanship. There are many pigeon-holes and drawers, cabinets and files, occupied by papers that have been assorted and classified.'[39] In 1900 it was estimated that the bishop received some five thousand communications a year.

The stables which had been rebuilt earlier in the century housed three horses in Dr Percival's time, 'two being used with the brougham, and a third, a fine docile creature, carrying his Lordship when circumstances favour riding.'[40] The bishop, for whom 'it was of frequent occurence ... to drive or ride twenty miles to some service or meeting' is remembered as the last to visit his diocese on horseback. There are those who can still remember the bishop's horses being led over the Wye bridge from the palace to the Bishop's Meadow opposite to graze. In 1914 Dr Percival vested the lease of this meadow in Hereford Corporation as a public space and playing field. In 1937 Charles Lisle Carr, 1931-1941, gave the city the meadow's freehold. The diocese was once well served by railways so the acquisition of an episcopal motor car, chauffeur, and garage, all of which were housed in the former stables, was slower in occuring than in other dioceses. There were few parishes in the diocese, despite its rural character, which could not be reached from Hereford by train.

At the turn of the century the palace was still a self-contained household. All its bread was baked on the premises and vaulted cellars housed its wine. The bishop has salmon rights over the Wye and his net sheds stand on the opposite bank to the palace. Extensive vegetable gardens provided the kitchen daily with fresh supplies. A complicated network of bell wires, vestiges of which are still to be seen in the roof above the great hall, summoned the domestic staff to their duties. Butler and housekeeper presided over the household's smooth running, and in living memory the tradition was that the butler ate with the servants in the evening and then joined the housekeeper, who ate alone, for a glass or two of port. For those at the other end of the house, socially and geographically, there were pleasure gardens, a tennis court, a crouquet lawn, and 'a picturesque dovecot', housing eighty pigeons.

VII. THE TWENTIETH CENTURY

The first bishop to be nominated to Hereford in the twentieth century was the controversial Herbert Hensley Henson, 1918-1920. He was, no doubt, somewhat surprised to discover his new home, despite its size, did not possess a single bathroom. He soon had this deficiency remedied and when he was translated to Durham in 1920 he bequeathed to his successor a palace which now had the luxury of two bathrooms. He was, no doubt, equally surprised to discover that if the roof gutters became blocked by Autumn leaves heavy rain was apt to flood the house. The cure of this inconvenience involved a costly reconstruction of the palace's roofing. The bishop also entirely relaid the palace's drainage system and had 'a good hot water system, previously absent, introduced.'[41] Finally, Hensley Henson provided for the first time access from the first floor of the kitchen wing, which hitherto had been quite separate, to the rest of the house.

The twentieth century has seen a continuing debate on the role of bishops in the contemporary Church and this, amongst other things, has involved a considerable amount of discussion about the part to be played in Church life by the bishop's house. Thus Archbishop Glyn Simon in his contribution to *Bishops,* 1961, a distinguished collection of essays which he also edited, wrote: 'It is not enough that bishops should live simply; they must be *seen* to live simply... Let the bishop live in a much smaller house, and let his office needs be seen and recognised for what they are, part of his official life which he cannot escape and which needs space in which to discharge it.' And so it is that the palace at Hereford has undergone a steady process of adaptation to a new role as not only the home of the diocesan bishop, but also of the growing diocesan administration.

The Church Commissioners took over the responsibility of the palace in 1946 and in the period 1949-51 undertook a major reconstruction. At some aesthetic cost, the most southern but one of the ground floor sash windows of Bisse's eighteenth century scheme was lost by being turned into the front door of a new bishop's house formed out of the south end of the main palace building. The former

Bisse's great hall after its restoration in 1975.

The palace from the Bishop's netting sheds, showing Victorian and 20th century alterations.

drawing room was divided once again into two rooms, this time a chapel and the bishop's study. The library became a secretaries' office. At the extreme southern end of the building, and at some further aesthetic cost, a small wing was built projecting into the courtyard to accommodate the domestic offices of this new bishop's house, the size of which was more realistically atuned to the needs and ideals of contemporary episcopal living. A suite of offices was made for the Diocesan Board of Finance at the north end of the building where the former episcopal dining room was turned into a conference room and three cottages were made out of the north range of buildings.

Unfortunately, two years later a further reconstruction was necessitated, debris having been noticed on the altar of the new palace chapel which aroused suspicions that all was not well with the medieval roof timbers and their supporting arches. Inspection revealed death watch beetle and both the dry and wet varieties of rot. Their successful eradication involved major engineering works, including the introduction steel girders, a new chapel ceiling, and the extensive chemical treatment of the timbers themselves. The progress of the work was reported in the *National Builder*[42] and the palace became the subject of rather sober advertisements in the building press promoting the excellence of the insecticides used in preserving its timbers: 'If you would like to be sure of solving your own problems of timber decay, write for a copy of *The Control of Insect and Fungal Destroyers of Timber.* This free technical brochure contains information of value to every Architect and Builder.' An innovation introduced in the course of this restoration was the installation of inspection panels so that scholars and students could study the surviving Norman wooden pillars supporting the palace roof. Thus, a section of a classical column on the north wall of the great hall, introduced as part of Bisse's restoration, can now be opened at the touch of a handle to reveal the twelfth century oak pillar it conceals.

In 1974 the appointment of John Eastaugh as bishop led to the restoration in the following year, as part of the celebrations for the thirteenth hundred anniversary of the foundation of the diocese, of the great hall and its transformation into one of the most handsome rooms in the city of Hereford. Yellow, white, and gold replaced dark brown and the heavy imitation stone blocks which disfigured the walls were replaced with smooth plaster; chandeliers and appropriate episcopal portraits were introduced, and the light and graceful spirit of Bisse's early eighteenth century great hall once again prevails. It provides an elegant domestic setting for recitals and gatherings of all kinds and has re-establishned the palace's cultural role in the life of Hereford.

The palace's library also enhances the city's intellectual resources. It contains the See Library of books and pamphlets on Herefordshire and Shropshire built up by successive bishops, and is an invaluable aid, augmented by a complete run of the *Transactions of the Woolhope Club* from 1862 to the present day, for local historians. The palace library also contains an extensive run of Crockford's *Clerical Directory.* From the first issue in 1858 to 1901 it is complete, being a gift from a one time editor who was a Herefordshire man. From 1929 to the present day only one volume is missing, and it is hoped eventually to establish a complete Crockford in the library.

Thus, the palace which does not make a show represents a continuous tradition of episcopal living stretching over eight hundred years. It has survived border wars, civil wars, and two world wars; it has adapted to innumerable religious, political, and social changes. Moreover, it has survived as a home for the bishops of Hereford. The number of ancient episcopal palaces which are still the homes of their bishops is declining rapidly. Their counterparts on the continent, especially in France, have often become town halls or museums, and nearer home the once handsome palace of the bishops of St Davids at Abergwili is now the county museum, and the bishops of Swansea and Brecon live in a bijou residence at Brecon. But set in its four acres of parkland sloping down to the Wye, the palace at Hereford continues to offer hospitality and Christian service to all who visit it, even to the swans gliding by on the river and the mallard ducks nesting and rearing their young on its lawns.

The Episcopal Occupants of the Palace at Hereford

Pre-Norman:

Putta,	676
Tyrhtel,	688
Torhthere,	710
Wahlstod,	c.720
Cuthberht,	736-740
Podda,	741
Acca,	c.747
Headda,	c.758
Aldberht,	777
Esne,	c.781
Ceolmund,	c.786
Utel,	c.793
Wulfheard,	c.799
Beonna,	824
Eadwulf,	c.825
Cuthwulf,	c.836
Mucel,	c.857
Deorlaf,	c.857
Cynemund,	888
Edgar,	c.888
Tidhelm,	930
Wulfhelm,	c.934
Aelfric,	c.934
Athwulf,	c.971
Aethelstan,	c.1013-1056
Leofgar,	1056
Ealdred, Bishop of Hereford & Worcester,	1056-1060
Walter,	1061-1079

Post-Norman:

Robert Losinga,	1079-1095
Gerard,	1096-1100
Reinhelm	1102-1115
Geoffrey	1115-1119
Richard de Capella	1121-1127
Robert de Bethune	1131-1148
Gilbert Foliot	1148-1163
Robert de Melun	1163-1167
Robert Foliot	1173-1186
William de Vere	1186-1198
Giles de Braose	1200-1215
Hugh de Mapenore	1216-1219
Hugh Foliot	1219-1234
Ralph Maidstone	1234-1239
Peter D'Aigueblanche	1240-1268
John Breton	1269-1275
Thomas Cantilupe	1275-1282
Richard Swinfield	1283-1317
Adam Orleton	1317-1327
Thomas Charlton	1327-1344
John Trilleck	1344-1360
Lewis Charlton	1361-1369
William Courtenay	1370-1375
John Gilbert	1375-1389
John Trefnant	1389-1404
Robert Mascall	1404-1416
Edmund Lacy	1417-1420
Thomas Polton	1420-1421
Thomas Spofford	1422-1448
Richard Beauchamp	1449-1450
Reginald Boulers	1450-1453
John Stanbury	1453-1474
Thomas Milling	1474-1492
Edmund Audley	1492-1502
Adriano de Castello	1502-1504
Richard Mayew	1504-1516
Charles Booth	1516-1535
Edward Fox	1535-1538
Edmund Bonner	1538-1539
John Skip	1539-1552

John Harley	1553-1554
Robert Parfew	1554-1557
Thomas Reynolds	1558-1559
John Scory	1559-1585
Herbert Westfaling	1586-1602
Robert Bennett	1603-1617
Francis Godwin	1617-1633
William Juxon	1633-1633
Augustine Lindsell	1634-1634
Matthew Wren	1635-1635
Theophilus Field	1635-1636
George Coke	1636-1646
Nicholas Monk	1661-1661
Herbert Croft	1662-1691
Gilbert Ironside	1691-1701
Humphrey Humphries	1701-1712
Philip Bisse	1713-1721
Benjamin Hoadly	1721-1723
Henry Egerton	1724-1746
James Beauclerk	1746-1787
John Harley	1787-1788
John Butler	1788-1802
Ffoliot Cornewall	1803-1808
John Luxmoore	1808-1815
George Huntingford	1815-1832
Edward Grey	1832-1837
Thomas Musgrave	1837-1847
Renn Dickson Hampden	1848-1868
James Atlay	1868-1894
John Percival	1895-1917
Herbert Hensley Henson	1918-1920
Martin Linton Smith	1920-1930
Charles Lisle Carr	1931-1941
Richard Parsons	1941-1948
Tom Longworth	1949-1961
Mark Hodson	1961-1973
John Eastaugh	1974-1990

NOTES

1. Nikolaus Pevsner, *Buildings of England: Herefordshire,* Harmondsworth, 1963, p 171.
2. Ibid, pp 171, 172.
3. R. W. D. Fenn, 'Early Christianity in Herefordshire', *Transactions of the Woolhope Naturalists' Field Club*, XXXIX, 1968, pt II, pp 333-345.
4. E. Ekwall, *The Concise Oxford Dictionary of English Place-names,* 4th ed, Oxford, 1960, p 236.
5. H. P. R. Finberg, ed, *Early Charters of the West Midlands,* Leicester, 1961, pp 127, 225-227.
6. Thomas Jones, ed, *Brut y Tywysogyon or the Chronicle of the Princes,* Red Book of Hergest Version, Cardiff, 1955, p 25.
7. J. E. Lloyd, *A History of Wales,* 3rd ed, London, 1939, pp 367, 368.
8. Cited by A. L. Moir, *The Bishops of Hereford, Their Cathedral and Palace,* Hereford, 1964, p 57.
9. *Brut y Tywysogyon,* p 159.
10. L. Toulmin Smith, ed, *Leland's Itinerary,* V, London, 1910. p. 184.
11. Ralegh Radford, Tonkin, and Jope, 'The Great Hall of the Bishop's Palace at Hereford', *Medieval Archaeology,* XVIII, 1973, p. 86.
12. John Blair, 'The 12th-Century Bishop's Palace at Hereford', *Medieval Archaeology,* XXXI, 1987, p 65.
13. Ibid, p 71.
14. Ibid, p 67.
15. *Brut y Tywysogyon,* p 203.
16. Ibid, p. 209.

17. Peter D'Aigueblanche was succeeded by John Breton, 1269-1275.
18. Bishop Orleton was succeeded by Thomas Charlton, 1327-1344.
19. Edmund Lacy's immediate successor was Thomas Polton, 1420-21.

20. Thomas Spofford was followed by Richard Beauchamp, 1449-50, and Reginald Boulers, 1450-53.
21. Thomas Milling was bishop from 1474-1492, Edmund Audley 1492-1502, and Adriano de Castello 1502-1504.
22. Blair, op. cit., p 71.
23. John Skip was succeeded by John Harley, 1553-54.
24. William Juxon, dean of Worcester, was nominated as Godwin's successor, but before his consecration was appointed to London and Geoffrey Goodman, bishop of Gloucester, though elected, never came to Hereford.
25. PRO: E. 179/119/492: we are grateful to Mr M. A. Faraday for this information.
26. Gilbert Ironside, 1691-1701, was his immediate successor.
27. F. T. Havergal, *Fasti Herefordenses,* Edinburgh, 1869, p 33.
28. This was later removed and is now in the bishop's chapel.
29. Plate IV in Blair, op. cit.
30. Report of W. D. Caroe, architect to Ecclesiastical Commissioners, October 1920.
31. Ibid, p 67.
32. Moir, *Bishops of Hereford,* p 60.
33. J. Jones, Junior, *Hereford, Cathedral and City,* Hereford, 1858, p. x.
34. J. Merewether, *Restoration of the Cathedral Church of Hereford,* London, 1842, p 6.
35. Frederick Dolman, 'Great Preachers, their homes and households: The Rt Revd John Percival and Mrs Percival', *The Sunday Strand,* 1900.
36. Ibid, In fact there were five of these windows, not six.
37. *Hereford Times,* September 12th, 1868.
38. Pevsner, op. cit., p 172.
39. Frederick Dolman, op. cit.
40. Ibid.
41. Caroe, op. cit.
42. *The National Builder,* XXXIV, 1954, pp 118, 119.